D0841109

Is Atheism Dead?

The Unbelieving Unbelievers
Epidemic

Book 1 of
"They Walk Among Us"
series

RSI
PUBLISHING

CHARLES W MORRIS

Scriptures are taken from the English Standard Version of the Bible

Books may be ordered through booksellers or by contacting:
RSIP
Raising the Standard International Publishing L. L. C.

RSIP-Charles Morris
https://www.rsiministry.com
Navarre, Florida

ISBN: 9781955830492
Printed in the United States of America
Edition Date: March 2022

CONTENTS

DEDICATION

I want to dedicate this book to all believers who at times scratch your head and wonder, "What in the world are people thinking?" You hear logic makes no logical sense, and you wonder if the world has gone completely mad. It seems to have departed from everything that resembles common sense and all sense of decency.

I dedicate this book to those of you who choose to stand with God in the power of the Holy Spirit and in the name that is above all names, our Lord Jesus Christ. My prayer for you as you read this is that you will be encouraged and strengthened to stand righteous in unrighteous times, to stand steadfast in times of untruth, and to stand in light in the times of darkness.

ACKNOWLEDGMENT

When writing "IS ATHEISM DEAD?" there are many people I can thank for their assistance, directly or indirectly. First and foremost, I thank my wife Debby, who patiently gives me the freedom to write all hours of the day and into the night as I receive ideas. This need for outside help is especially true when the book is the first in a series of four.

Writing and publishing coaches say that any book worth its salt has an editor and proofreader behind it. I want to thank Mrs. Cathy Cay Campbell Sleeth, who read through the final draft and cleaned up mistakes that I had read over numerous times and missed. I also thank her for writing the first review for this book. Thank you, Cathy.

I love the discovery of Biblical facts on hard subjects. Words of wisdom spoken so I can have understanding. Waiting very impatiently for the rest of the books.
Cathy Cay Campbell Sleeth

I also want to thank author Terry Scott who has been standing with my ministry since 2001. He also read through "IS ATHEISM DEAD?" and wrote a review. Thank you, Terry.

This book is a must-read for all. Charles once again explains just how much we must be on our guard to what we believe and follow in the last remaining day before the return of the Lord Jesus Christ. He has expressed just how much atheism has infected the whole world, including the church. What type of believer are you? Charles answers this question and follows through with a biblical explanation of how far the church has drifted from believing in the Lord Jesus Christ. We are in the last days, and Charles has explained how the antichrist has rooted in the church and infected the body of Christ, setting it up for the last days, falling away from the Truth of God's Word.

Author Terry Scott

CHAPTER 1
INTRODUCTION

Is Atheism Dead? It may seem that way, and yet they walk among us. The masses are not walking around with a tee-shirt, stating, "I am an atheist. A simple glance at books, movies, and social media would certainly tell us, "No, atheism is not dead." Oh, it might be renamed and dressed up in a prettier and more sophisticated package with a modern "Gnostic" or "Humanistic" title, but atheism is alive and well on planet earth.

Who are these atheists, what do they typically believe, and more importantly, how does all of this affect my family and me? We know from reading Scriptures that as we edge closer to the end of the times as we know them, the antichrist spirit will increase in presence, strength, and demonic activity.

Since a group walks among us called "the atheists," whom I will address as the *"Unbelieving Unbelievers,"* what are the classifications of the other three groups of people?

"Is Atheism Dead? The Unbelieving Unbeliever" is book 1 of the "They Walk Among Us" series. These books show the four

classifications of people, their typical belief system, behavioral patterns, and a warning for true believers.

Many would look at the Scriptures and say there are only two types of people, those who are spiritually lost and those who are spiritually saved. This assessment is very accurate and Biblical. However, the Scriptures divide these two classes into four groups that I call the four types or classifications of people. There are two types of unbelievers and two types of believers.

After reading each of my books, you will need to assess which classification you fall into and what God says about it. There is certainly enough Biblical evidence to divide the lost into two groups and divide the saved into two groups. The four groups are listed below.

THE UNBELIEVING UNBELIEVER (a spiritually lost person, known as an atheist)

THE BELIEVING UNBELIEVER (a spiritually lost person, known as the religiously lost)

THE UNBELIEVING BELIEVER (a spiritually saved person, known as the saved, satisfied, and spiritually immature)

THE BELIEVING BELIEVER (a spiritually saved person, known as the Mark

16:16-20. These believers are spiritually armed and dangerous to the kingdom of darkness.)

These four types can make life interesting when they collide in the everyday workplace, church, or home. They even collide in our day-to-day shopping experiences and on the roadways while driving. That is why we see road rage and people fighting in department stores. The days of having a "safe haven" have ended.

There are four books in this "They Walk Among Us" series. In these four short books, I will give Scripture teaching on each, and hopefully, we can have a self-assessment to identify which group we find ourselves in. Once we know where we stand spiritually, I hope to show how we all can move to the fourth position of being a *Believing Believer*" and remain there.

If we are in the fourth group, we need to minister to the first three groups while having sweet fellowship with others in group number four. If we are in the fourth group and attempt to fellowship with the first three, we are in danger of drifting away from the faith. The Word of God tells us we are in the world, but we are not of the world.

Before jumping deep into the book, let's look at how atheists stack up in American culture. The number of people who embrace atheism grows each year. Americans who identified themselves as atheists have increased significantly to around five percent of the population in the past decade. Atheists make up a larger share of the people in many European countries than in the U.S. In most European countries, atheists make up 15 to 19 percent of the population. So you see that we have a silent epidemic that affects all of society while each culture is shifting towards being amoral.

The basic literal definition of an "atheist" is a person who does not believe in the existence of a god or any gods. In the U.S., 68 percent of atheists are young men, and of those, 78 percent are highly educated white men.

Most atheists are not concerned one way or another about the religions of others. The vast majority, or 93 percent of U.S. atheists, say religion is not essential in their lives. So, where do atheists find meaning in life? Like most Americans, most atheists mentioned family life as the source of the importance of life. However, atheists were far more likely than Christians to describe hobbies as meaningful or satisfying. Twenty-six percent say they found a significant source of happiness in their hobbies.

For the most part, being an atheist isn't just about personally rejecting religious labels and beliefs. The majority of atheists express strong negative views when asked about the role of religion in society. For example, 71 percent of U.S. atheists say religion's influence is declining in American public life and that this is a good thing. Atheists may not believe in any religious teachings, but they are well informed on most religious organizations, creeds, and statements of faith. Fifty-six percent of Americans say it is not necessary to believe in God to be moral, while 42 percent say belief in God is necessary to possess good Biblical values.

Think about how these statements affect us who believe in God and the Bible. If I am an atheist and think that religion is one of the problems in society, then I would spend time and resources to eradicate it from everyday life.

Currently, Americans as a whole do not feel socially warm toward atheists than they do toward members of most major religious groups. U.S. adults relate or feel towards atheists the same as they do towards Muslims.

Okay, now that we have some basic understanding of atheism in America, let's get down to business. Let's look at what God says about the **Unbelieving Unbeliever**. Follow me as we answer the question, "Is Atheism Dead?"

CHAPTER 2
THE UNBELIEVING
UNBELIEVER
(The Atheist)

The *Unbelieving Unbeliever* is the first group of people we will identify in the world. Who are they, what do they believe, and how does this affect my family and me?

The *Unbelieving Unbeliever* is the person who, from his heart, acknowledges that there is no God. The *Unbelieving Unbeliever* is the spiritually lost person, who may or may not claim to be an atheist, but certainly has an atheist's traits, lifestyle, and mindset. They are heart-hardened towards the Gospel message and, according to the Scriptures, are fools and liars. Don't get me wrong; they can be recognized as moral people in their culture. However, their culture is far removed from the morals and guidelines of God's Word and nature. In other words, their morality is to do what is right in their own eyes.

There is a false confession in which the words spoken do not agree with the heart's belief. Some confess with their mouths that they are Christians yet are atheists in their hearts. These seek to deceive undiscerning

Is Atheism Dead?

Christians and win their attention, acceptance, and trust. We see this often in politics as some politicians claim to know God to win the vote of Christians while possessing a hardened unbelieving heart.

There will be those who confess with their mouths that they do not believe in the existence of God. However, their hearts are not true to their confession. They may admit they do not believe in God's existence for many reasons. It could be the desire to live an immoral lifestyle with their sinful friends without fear of being laughed at or rejected.

In the early summer of 1974, when I was spiritually lost and heavily involved with drugs, a group of my drug buddies was visiting Myrtle Beach, South Carolina. We were standing on the beach watching the sunrise after "partying" all night. While watching the beauty of the dawn, suddenly out of my mouth came the proclamation, "Look at what beauty God has given us." Those with me all claimed to be atheists with their confession, but it "bummed" them out when I made that statement. One guy asked, "Man, why did you have to say that?" They were atheists by admission, but they still believed there was a God in their minds, and the Holy Spirit was dealing with them as He was with me. I was born again six months later.

The true **Unbelieving Unbelievers** are those whose hearts are seared and hardened and have no conviction of the Holy Spirit. These people quickly deny the existence of God, are not convicted of their sin and have no reservations of laughing or mocking those who do believe.

CHAPTER 3
THE UNBELIEVING
UNBELIEVER IS WICKED AND
A FOOL

For the reader's convenience, I will list the traits of the *Unbelieving Unbeliever or the atheist* at the beginning of each chapter.

The *Unbelieving Unbeliever*
1. Is wicked and a fool

The Word of God is quick to classify certain types of people, like those who fear God are considered wise. These classifications are not "man's" opinions about people but how God Himself distinguishes His creation. God warns us of arbitrary calling someone a fool. For our knowledge, He identifies who is truly a fool.

The Bible clearly states that the *Unbelieving Unbeliever* is a fool and is wicked. But what are the characteristics or attributes of a wicked and foolish person according to the Bible? God says that the fool and the wicked claim there is no God.

When we think of someone as wicked, we say they have a moral and depraved lifestyle. We would say the wicked are disposed to or marked by mischief or disgustingly unpleasant. Wicked could also be identified as someone causing or likely to cause harm, distress, or trouble. We would identify the wicked as bad, dark, evil, immoral, nefarious, rotten, sinful, unethical, unlawful, unrighteous, vicious, vile, villainous, criminal, and wrong.

When we think of someone as a fool, we would typically say it is a person who acts unwisely or imprudently or a silly person. A fool is a person without good sense or judgment, lacking in the common powers of understanding. We might use synonyms for a fool such as cuckoo, ding-a-ling, dingbat, dipstick, doofus, half-wit, lunatic, nincompoop, nitwit, nutcase, simpleton, or a yo-yo. Furthermore, we might use terms for a fool like one who is absurd, asinine, brainless, bubbleheaded, crackpot, crazy, daffy, dippy, feather-headed, foolish, half-baked, half-witted, harebrained, inept, insane, kooky, loony, lunatic, mad, nutty, screwball, senseless, silly, simpleminded, stupid, weak-minded, and witless. You may have used some of these words to identify someone, or maybe someone used a few of these phrases to identify you.

However, God calls people wicked and fools because they reject Him in their minds and hearts. And because someone denies the existence of God, they are called corrupt in their words, deeds, and thoughts.

> *Psalms 14:1 (ESV) To the choirmaster. Of David. The fool says in his heart, "There is no God." They are corrupt, they do abominable deeds; there is none who does good.*

The Hebrew word fool in Psalms 14:1 is "nabal" (H5036) and is translated as stupid, wicked, vile, and foolish. This word is used 18 times in the Old Testament. (For more study, see Deuteronomy 32:6; 32:21; 2 Samuel 3:33; 13:13; Job 30:8; Isaiah 32:5-6; Jeremiah 17:11; Ezekiel 13:3).

> *Psalms 10:4 (ESV) In the pride of his face the wicked does not seek him; all his thoughts are, "There is no God."*

> *Psalms 53:1-4 (ESV) To the choirmaster: according to Mahalath. A Maskil of David. The fool says in his heart, "There is no God." They are corrupt, doing abominable iniquity; there is none who does good. 2 God looks down from heaven on the children of man to see if there are any who understand, who seek after God. 3 They have all fallen*

away; together they have become corrupt; there is none who does good, not even one. 4 Have those who work evil no knowledge, who eat up my people as they eat bread, and do not call upon God?

The Hebrew word wicked in Psalms 10:4 is "rasha" (H7563) and is translated as morally wrong, an actively bad person, condemned, guilty, ungodly, and wicked. This word is used 263 times in the Old Testament.

Psalms 39:7-8 (ESV) "And now, O Lord, for what do I wait? My hope is in you. 8 Deliver me from all my transgressions. Do not make me the scorn of the fool!

Psalms 74:18 (ESV) Remember this, O LORD, how the enemy scoffs, and a foolish people reviles your name.

Psalms 74:22 (ESV) Arise, O God, defend your cause; remember how the foolish scoff at you all the day!

Proverbs 17:7 (ESV) Fine speech is not becoming to a fool; still less is false speech to a prince.

When the Bible says they are fools, meaning stupid, it does not mean they are uneducated by worldly standards. They could be incredibly intelligent and acclaimed in the world of academia. The apostle Paul, who was highly educated, claimed that he counted all his worldly knowledge as camel dung or rubbish for the sake of knowing Christ.

Philippians 3:7-8 (ESV) But whatever gain I had, I counted as loss for the sake of Christ. 8 Indeed, I count everything as loss because of the surpassing worth of knowing Christ Jesus my Lord. For his sake I have suffered the loss of all things and count them as rubbish, in order that I may gain Christ

To the foolish *Unbelieving Unbeliever* or the atheist, the preaching of the cross is folly. God says that He would destroy all of man's worldly wisdom, and they would look foolish.

1 Corinthians 1:18-21 (ESV) For the word of the cross is folly to those who are perishing, but to us who are being saved it is the power of God. 19 For it is written, "I will destroy the wisdom of the wise, and the discernment of the discerning I will thwart." 20 Where is the one who is wise? Where is the scribe? Where is the debater of this age? Has not God made foolish the wisdom of the world? 21 For since, in the wisdom of God, the world did not know God through wisdom, it pleased God through the folly of what we preach to save those who believe.

How does this affect us? One of the most noticeable areas in which we who believe are affected by **Unbelieving Unbelievers** would be their illogical decisions and mandates. In all of their "so-called" intelligence, expertise, and wisdom, their plans, decisions, mandates, and laws make no logical sense and are a contradiction. Their findings are based on greed and control. In this drive to gain more financial wealth and power, they seek to instill fear upon the masses while belittling anyone who stands against their irrational logic.

God says He would take those not politically, financially, or educationally positioned in this world and exalt them in Christ to confound the strong and wise. He would take those considered weak and foolish to shame the strong and wise. God chose the low and despised to bring the things exalted by mankind to nothing. He did this so that all men have nothing to boast in except the righteousness of Christ.

1 Corinthians 1:25-31 (ESV) For the foolishness of God is wiser than men, and the weakness of God is stronger than men. 26 For consider your calling, brothers: not many of you were wise according to worldly standards, not many were powerful, not many were of noble birth. 27 But God chose what is foolish in the world to shame the wise; God chose what is weak in the world to shame the strong; 28 God chose what is low and despised in the world, even things that are not, to bring to nothing things that are, 29 so that no human being might boast in the presence of God. 30 And because of him you are in Christ Jesus, who became to us wisdom from God, righteousness and sanctification and redemption, 31 so that, as it is written, "Let the one who boasts, boast in the Lord."

CHAPTER 4
THE UNBELIEVING UNBELIEVER OR THE FOOL IS RIGHT IN HIS OWN EYES

The *Unbelieving Unbeliever*
1. Is wicked and a fool
2. Is right in his own eyes

Although God calls *Unbelieving Unbelievers* fools, they see themselves as being wise and right in their eyes. In my book "A Willingness To Be Taught," I describe those who are dull of hearing and those who no longer have ears to hear. Of course, I am not speaking about physical hearing. I am talking about those who have spiritual ears to hear spiritual truths versus those who no longer hear spiritual truths.

If you have tried to speak to someone who no longer has spiritual ears to hear, then you know they can be very argumentative because they are always right in their own eyes. They refuse to be persuaded by the facts. Only a foolish man would argue with a fool. In contrast, the wise man seeks and gives an ear to advice.

Is Atheism Dead?

Proverbs 12:15-16 (ESV) The way of a fool is right in his own eyes, but a wise man listens to advice. 16 The vexation of a fool is known at once, but the prudent ignores an insult.

The Hebrew word fool in Proverbs 12:15-16 is "eviyl" (H191) and is pronounced ev-eel. It is the root where we get our English word evil. It is translated as perverse, silly, and foolish. This word is used 26 times in the Old Testament. (For more study, see Job 5:2-3; Proverbs 7:22; 10:8; 10:14; 10:21; 12:16; 14:3; 11:29; 12:15; 14:9; 15:5; 16:22; 17:28; 20:3; 24:7; 27:3; 27:22; 29:9; Isaiah 19:11; 35:8; Jeremiah 4:22; and Hosea 9:7).

Notice in Proverbs 12:16 the phrase "The vexation of a fool is known at once." Vexation is anger, grief, indignation, provocation, spite, and wrath. These attributes mean the foolish are quick-tempered.

So, how does this attitude affect us? Have you noticed the anger and rage people have everywhere now? Because of road rage, some are becoming afraid to drive our highways. Even as I was writing this section, I witnessed the road rage of a driver making a wrong decision that almost caused an accident. The person who was nearly hit blew the horn in a long continuous blow, which some of us would have done in this situation. But then he

17

cut off the other car, got out, and began to scream at the lady who made the driving error. This action was unnecessarily cruel and revealed the nature and heart of the person. In essence, he was saying that he has never made a driving error; therefore, he has the right to attack anyone who does verbally.

Folks are losing control of their emotions in grocery stores, food courts, shopping malls, and just about any venue where people gather for business or pleasure.

Because of this notion of being right in their own eyes, they become impatient, hostile, and feel they are above the constraints of the law. They feel a sense of entitlement that they have the right to say, do, or take whatever they please because it is owed to them. Everything someone does affects others in some way. No man is an island to himself.

Romans 14:7 (ESV) For none of us lives to himself, and none of us dies to himself.

Psalms 107:17 (ESV) Some were fools through their sinful ways, and because of their iniquities suffered affliction;

Psalms 107:17 is another way of saying what God's Word told us in Galatians 6:7-8, that we reap what we sow. The best translation of Psalms 107:17 resembles some of the metaphors commonly used, such as "what goes around comes around." Other metaphors on this matter are "He brought this upon himself," and "He made his bed, let him lie in it." These metaphors mean that we must face the consequences of our actions. We should be intentional in making good decisions in treating others with patience and kindness then we will receive the same from others.

> **Galatians 6:7-8 (ESV) Do not be deceived: God is not mocked, for whatever one sows, that will he also reap. 8 For the one who sows to his own flesh will from the flesh reap corruption, but the one who sows to the Spirit will from the Spirit reap eternal life.**
>
> **Proverbs 1:7 (ESV) The fear of the LORD is the beginning of knowledge; fools despise wisdom and instruction.**

In King Solomon's later years, he failed to follow his own advice. He did not pursue wisdom but was foolish, and we see the tragic results in the Book of Ecclesiastes. Solomon was a man who had everything in life that anybody could wish for, and yet felt emptiness and was frustrated with his life. He was a man who had everything and yet had nothing.

> **Proverbs 12:16 (ESV) The vexation of a fool is known at once, but the prudent ignores an insult.**

Try to instruct a fool, and he'll hate you. A fool's wrath is quickly known. Because they are right in their own eyes, they quickly spout off their mouths. They are quick to "give you a piece of their minds." They fail in giving grace and do not try to hide their displeasure. A good man will let an insult go.

We have an abundance of vehicles on our roadways today. People are going to get distracted and make bad driving decisions. This precarious situation is not the time to be foolish and enter into road rage to inform someone of their error. The fool cannot restrain his wrath when he is vexed. Just because you might feel you are always right does not mean everyone else accepts that they are as perfect as you are.

> **Proverbs 25:28 (ESV) A man without self-control is like a city broken into and left without walls.**

> **James 1:19-20 (ESV) Know this, my beloved brothers: let every person be quick to hear, slow to speak, slow to**

anger; 20 for the anger of man does not produce the righteousness of God.

What should we do? First, we need to learn to give mercy and grace to people. We also need to know that we are not to be friends with *Unbelieving Unbelievers*, lest we find ourselves walking in their sins.

Proverbs 22:24-25 (ESV) Make no friendship with a man given to anger, nor go with a wrathful man, 25 lest you learn his ways and entangle yourself in a snare.

Psalms 1:1 (ESV) Blessed is the man who walks not in the counsel of the wicked, nor stands in the way of sinners, nor sits in the seat of scoffers;

1 Corinthians 15:33 (ESV) Do not be deceived: "Bad company ruins good morals."

CHAPTER 5
THE UNBELIEVING
UNBELIEVER OR THE FOOL
DESPISES UNDERSTANDING
AND WISDOM

The *Unbelieving Unbeliever*
1. Is wicked and a fool
2. Is right in his own eyes
3. Despises understanding and wisdom

We covered some of this in the last chapter in seeing that the *Unbelieving Unbeliever* is right in his own eyes. We will now look closer at how the *Unbelieving Unbeliever* or the atheist despises understanding and wisdom. Their attitude is, "don't try to confuse me with the facts." They are greatly deceived and find it easier to believe a lie over the truth. We know this is true by how our false news media influences the masses.

> **Proverbs 1:7 (ESV) The fear of the LORD is the beginning of knowledge; fools despise wisdom and instruction.**

Is Atheism Dead?

The Hebrew word fool in Proverbs 1:7 is the same as Proverbs 12:15-16. It is translated as perverse, silly, and foolish.

Proverbs 18:2 (ESV) A fool takes no pleasure in understanding, but only in expressing his opinion.

Proverbs 23:9 (ESV) Do not speak in the hearing of a fool, for he will despise the good sense of your words.

The Hebrew word fool in Proverbs 18:2 and 29:9 is "kesiyl" (H3684) and is pronounced kes-eel. It is translated as stupid or silly. This word is used seventy times in the Old Testament.

Again, the term stupid does not mean the *Unbelieving Unbeliever* is unlearned. Some of the more intelligent people I know are atheists or *Unbelieving Unbelievers*. They are profoundly acquainted with and well-versed in academia and far more knowledgeable in the things of the world than I will ever be. They are highly experienced, practiced, skilled, and scholarly.

However, they are ever learning but unable to come to the knowledge of the truth. Why? Because they lack understanding and wisdom from God. Since they deny the existence of God, they cannot draw from Him. God says that although they are wise in their own eyes, they are fools.

2 Timothy 3:7 (ESV) always learning and never able to arrive at a knowledge of the truth.

How does this affect us who believe? What can we glean from these Scriptures? God has given us who believe the opportunity to gain His wisdom and understanding. The Father has truths that He will hide from those who are atheists and give to those who believe. The most foolish person in the kingdom of God is wiser than the greatest intellectual who rejects God.

Matthew 13:10-11 (ESV) Then the disciples came and said to him, "Why do you speak to them in parables?" 11 And he answered them, "To you it has been given to know the secrets of the kingdom of heaven, but to them it has not been given.

We need to remember that the Holy Spirit takes people to Christ. Our Lord Jesus Christ brings us to the Father. When atheists deny God, they deny the work of Jesus. When they deny Jesus, they deny the work of the

Holy Spirit. Then their wisdom is null and void and declared foolishness by God.

1 Corinthians 1:19-21 (ESV) For it is written, "I will destroy the wisdom of the wise, and the discernment of the discerning I will thwart." 20 Where is the one who is wise? Where is the scribe? Where is the debater of this age? Has not God made foolish the wisdom of the world? 21 For since, in the wisdom of God, the world did not know God through wisdom, it pleased God through the folly of what we preach to save those who believe.

1 Corinthians 1:23-30 (ESV) but we preach Christ crucified, a stumbling block to Jews and folly to Gentiles, 24 but to those who are called, both Jews and Greeks, Christ the power of God and the wisdom of God. 25 For the foolishness of God is wiser than men, and the weakness of God is stronger than men. 26 For consider your calling, brothers: not many of you were wise according to worldly standards, not many were powerful, not many were of noble birth. 27 But God chose what is foolish in the world to shame the wise; God chose what is weak in the world to shame the strong; 28 God chose what is low

25

and despised in the world, even things that are not, to bring to nothing things that are, 29 so that no human being might boast in the presence of God. 30 And because of him you are in Christ Jesus, who became to us wisdom from God, righteousness and sanctification and redemption,

CHAPTER 6
THE UNBELIEVING
UNBELIEVER OR THE FOOL
SPEAKS HIS DESTRUCTION

The *Unbelieving Unbeliever*
1. Is wicked and a fool
2. Is right in his own eyes
3. Despises understanding and wisdom
4. Speaks destruction to his soul

I know this list reveals many negative attributes for the *Unbelieving Unbeliever,* but God is seriously against those who say He does not exist. We know the Scriptures teach us that out of the mouth comes life or death and blessing or cursing.

James 3:7-12 (ESV) For every kind of beast and bird, of reptile and sea creature, can be tamed and has been tamed by mankind, 8 but no human being can tame the tongue. It is a restless evil, full of deadly poison. 9 With it we bless our Lord and Father, and with it we curse people who are made in the likeness of God. 10 From the same mouth come blessing and cursing. My brothers, these things

27

> ***ought not to be so. 11 Does a spring pour forth from the same opening both fresh and salt water? 12 Can a fig tree, my brothers, bear olives, or a grapevine produce figs? Neither can a salt pond yield fresh water.***

Notice in James 3:10 that we can either bless or curse people. The tongue releases power. People would say to me, "That is a crazy idea." However, those same people have had their mood changed, become sick to their stomach, and sometimes have their blood pressure rise just because of a verbal attack.

We may have heard the phrase, "Caution: Be sure your brain is engaged before putting your mouth in gear." As Psalms 50:19 states, we often give our mouth too much freedom. The words of the *Unbelieving Unbeliever* are words that trap him like a curse and like death.

> ***Psalms 50:19 (ESV) "You give your mouth free rein for evil, and your tongue frames deceit.***

> ***Proverbs 18:7 (ESV) A fool's mouth is his ruin, and his lips are a snare to his soul.***

The Hebrew word for fool in Proverbs 18:7 is "kesiyl," the same as Proverbs 18:2 and

28

29:9. It is translated as stupid or silly. This word is used seventy times in the Old Testament. The apostle Paul has a lot to say concerning the *Unbelieving Unbeliever.*

Romans 3:10-18 (ESV) as it is written: "None is righteous, no, not one; 11 no one understands; no one seeks for God. 12 All have turned aside; together they have become worthless; no one does good, not even one." 13 "Their throat is an open grave; they use their tongues to deceive." "The venom of asps is under their lips." 14 "Their mouth is full of curses and bitterness." 15 "Their feet are swift to shed blood; 16 in their paths are ruin and misery, 17 and the way of peace they have not known." 18 "There is no fear of God before their eyes."

In Proverbs 18:21, we read that life and death are in the tongue.

Proverbs 18:21 (ESV) Death and life are in the power of the tongue, and those who love it will eat its fruits.

False prophets come bringing destruction by speaking their false message that there is no God or that we are our own gods. Remember that we will know the root by the fruit. The Scriptures tell us that one's words will condemn them.

> **Matthew 7:15-20 (ESV) "Beware of false prophets, who come to you in sheep's clothing but inwardly are ravenous wolves. 16 You will recognize them by their fruits. Are grapes gathered from thornbushes, or figs from thistles? 17 So, every healthy tree bears good fruit, but the diseased tree bears bad fruit. 18 A healthy tree cannot bear bad fruit, nor can a diseased tree bear good fruit. 19 Every tree that does not bear good fruit is cut down and thrown into the fire. 20 Thus you will recognize them by their fruits.**

How does this affect us? What can we do against the false message of eternal death that comes from the atheist? First, we need to believe God over man. Faith comes by hearing and hearing by the Word of God. We need to build up our faith by staying in the Word of God. Realize that God is for you. Separate yourselves from bad company. Love them by praying for them and blessing them when they attack you.

Is Atheism Dead?

1 Peter 3:9-12 (ESV) Do not repay evil for evil or reviling for reviling, but on the contrary, bless, for to this you were called, that you may obtain a blessing. 10 For "Whoever desires to love life and see good days, let him keep his tongue from evil and his lips from speaking deceit; 11 let him turn away from evil and do good; let him seek peace and pursue it. 12 For the eyes of the Lord are on the righteous, and his ears are open to their prayer. But the face of the Lord is against those who do evil."

Romans 12:14 (ESV) Bless those who persecute you; bless and do not curse them.

31

CHAPTER 7
THE UNBELIEVING
UNBELIEVER OR THE FOOL
CALLS GOD A LIAR

The *Unbelieving Unbeliever*
1. Is wicked and a fool
2. Is right in his own eyes
3. Despises understanding and wisdom
4. Speaks destruction to his soul
5. He calls God a liar by his own confession

1 John 5:10 (ESV) Whoever believes in the Son of God has the testimony in himself. Whoever does not believe God has made him a liar, because he has not believed in the testimony that God has borne concerning his Son.

We typically identify a liar as someone who continually speaks untruth. Anyone who does not believe God's report that Jesus Christ is God in the flesh continually calls God a liar. The apostle John in 1 John 5:10 calls *Unbelieving Unbelievers* or atheists' liars.

God says that the liars are those who do not believe God's testimony. Therefore, all who confess that Jesus Christ is not God are liars, meaning their whole lives are based on untruth. The typical atheist or *Unbelieving Unbeliever* redefines sin for his own wellbeing.

Since atheists don't believe in any gods, and sin exists only within the notion of gods, sin doesn't exist for atheists. So, atheists do not define sin from their point of view but redefine sin from the Bible's point of view. In other words, they would reject the notion of sin and are amoral in practice. Atheists believe that morals are a matter of each person's choice, and there should not be an absolute standard like the Bible. They would say that there is no defined right and wrong unless the action was against someone else. They would not call rape or murder a sin but a wrong choice.

Since atheists don't believe that Jesus was or is God nor that He "defeated death," they obviously don't believe that "Jesus saves them from sin." They know this concept of eternal redemption is fundamental to Christians and for an excellent reason. They would say that "freedom from sin" is a powerful freedom not to be scoffed at.

The Christian, however, does not say that we are free from sin. We say that we are free from the penalty and power of sin. We will not be free from the presence of sin until the end of all things that we know now, and our

Lord Jesus has established His Kingdom on the new earth. The atheists or *Unbelieving Unbelievers* would say all of this is just a fantasy that Christians need as a crutch to get through life. This allegation, again, is calling God a liar.

The atheists can't help themselves because even though they are not religious as we would call religion, according to John 8:44, their spiritual father is Satan. Just because someone doesn't believe in something does not make it false. Heaven and hell do not cease to exist just because atheists deny their existence. Jesus called this group of people liars because they rejected the truth.

> **John 8:54-55 (ESV) Jesus answered, "If I glorify myself, my glory is nothing. It is my Father who glorifies me, of whom you say, 'He is our God.' 55 But you have not known him. I know him. If I were to say that I do not know him, I would be a liar like you, but I do know him and I keep his word.**
>
> **John 8:42-47 (ESV) Jesus said to them, "If God were your Father, you would love me, for I came from God and I am here. I came not of my own accord, but he sent me. 43 Why do you not understand what I say? It is**

because you cannot bear to hear my word. 44 You are of your father the devil, and your will is to do your father's desires. He was a murderer from the beginning, and does not stand in the truth, because there is no truth in him. When he lies, he speaks out of his own character, for he is a liar and the father of lies. 45 But because I tell the truth, you do not believe me. 46 Which one of you convicts me of sin? If I tell the truth, why do you not believe me? 47 Whoever is of God hears the words of God. The reason why you do not hear them is that you are not of God. "

How does this mindset of the atheist affect us? What benefit do I gain in realizing that atheists operate from a deceptive philosophy? We must guard our hearts so that we do not fall into their trap. I will pick a topic and show the current mindset of American adults. I chose the topic of hell because there are seven times most Biblical references to hell and eternal judgment in God's Word than there are concerning heaven. The "spirit of antichrist," one of the spirit's controlling atheism, attacks and deceives people concerning any afterlife judgment.

Only 58 percent of adults in America believe in hell. That is not so alarming as the survey that showed only 82 percent of evangelical protestants and 60 percent of mainline protestants believe in the existence of hell. This alarming statistic means that many professing Christians have been deceived by believing the enemy's lies in denying God's Word concerning His judgment.

How does this atheistic mindset affect our next generation? Between the ages of 18-29, only 21 percent believe in the existence of hell. Think about it. That means 79 percent of 18-to-29-year-olds have no conviction or concern of God's judgment for their sin.

They say the political party you belong to does not affect you. However, the survey revealed that 54 percent of the democratic party does not believe in hell. What does this mean? First, they call God a liar, saying the Word of God is incorrect in its teaching, and assuming they are more competent concerning the afterlife than God. Secondly, if they deny God's Word on the existence of hell, how much more truth will they deny in order to fit their agenda?

> **Romans 3:3-4 (ESV) What if some were unfaithful? Does their faithlessness nullify the faithfulness of God? 4 By no means! Let God be true though every one were a liar, as it is written, "That you may be**

justified in your words, and prevail when you are judged."

CHAPTER 8
THE UNBELIEVING
UNBELIEVER OR THE FOOL IS
POTENTIALLY VIOLENT

The *Unbelieving Unbeliever*
1. Is wicked and a fool
2. Is right in his own eyes
3. Despises understanding and wisdom
4. Speaks destruction to his soul
5. He calls God a liar by his own confession
6. Is violent in nature

Psalms 94:3-6 (ESV) O LORD, how long shall the wicked, how long shall the wicked exult? 4 They pour out their arrogant words; all the evildoers boast. 5 They crush your people, O LORD, and afflict your heritage. 6 They kill the widow and the sojourner, and murder the fatherless;

The Hebrew word wicked in Psalms 94:3 is the same as in Psalms 10:4, which we read earlier. The word is "rasha" (H7563) translated as morally wrong, an actively bad person, condemned, guilty, ungodly, and wicked. This word is used 263 times in the Old Testament.

Does this mean that all atheists are violent? No, maybe not at the moment, but they have the great potential to be violent. Given the opportunity and their backs are against the wall, they will become that way. When people do not believe in God and His Word, they cast off restraint. In other words, they will do what pleases them at the moment, no matter how it affects others.

> **Proverbs 29:18 (ESV) Where there is no prophetic vision the people cast off restraint, but blessed is he who keeps the law.**

The Scriptures say they will cry out "Peace, peace" in the last days, but there will be no peace. In fact, our Lord Jesus Christ says that our enemies will come from our own homes.

> **Matthew 10:34-36 (ESV) "Do not think that I have come to bring peace to the earth. I have not come to bring peace, but a sword. 35 For I have come to set a man against his father, and a daughter against her mother, and a daughter-in-law against her mother-in-law. 36 And a person's enemies will be those of his own household.**

Many Scriptures reveal that **Unbelieving Unbelievers** or atheists will see Christians as their enemy and will attack them fiercely as they did in the first century. We will see a return of the hateful and murdering attitude of Haman from the Book of Esther.

> ***Psalms 14:2-4 (ESV) The LORD looks down from heaven on the children of man, to see if there are any who understand, who seek after God. 3 They have all turned aside; together they have become corrupt; there is none who does good, not even one. 4 Have they no knowledge, all the evildoers who eat up my people as they eat bread and do not call upon the LORD?***

> ***Esther 7:4-6 (ESV) For we have been sold, I and my people, to be destroyed, to be killed, and to be annihilated. If we had been sold merely as slaves, men and women, I would have been silent, for our affliction is not to be compared with the loss to the king." 5 Then King Ahasuerus said to Queen Esther, "Who is he, and where is he, who has dared to do this?" 6 And Esther said, "A foe and enemy! This wicked***

Haman!" Then Haman was terrified before the king and the queen.

But what has this got to do with us who believe? How will we remain righteous in such unrighteous times? We need to remind ourselves of the promises of God. Though we will be hated, attacked, persecuted, imprisoned, and killed, we will overcome. Those who are puffed up in their arrogance and unbelief now will be brought low. Those who dare to touch God's anointed children to harm them will be cast out into judgment.

There are hundreds of Scriptures in the New Testament concerning the end times judgment upon the unrighteous. However, in all that he suffered at the hands of so-called friends, Job gives us a concise overview of how God will balance the books. Take the time to read through these Scriptures and pray for those you know who profess to be atheists. Pray that they would have eyes to see and ears to hear God's truth as outlined within the pages of His Word. There will be more on our need to have spiritual ears to hear in the next chapter.

Job 20:4-7 (ESV) Do you not know this from of old, since man was placed on earth, 5 that the exulting of the wicked is short, and the joy of the godless but for a moment? 6 Though his height mount up to the heavens, and his head reach to the clouds, 7 he will perish forever like his own dung; those who have seen him will say, 'Where is he?'

Job 20:8-23 (ESV) He will fly away like a dream and not be found; he will be chased away like a vision of the night. 9 The eye that saw him will see him no more, nor will his place any more behold him. 10 His children will seek the favor of the poor, and his hands will give back his wealth. 11 His bones are full of his youthful vigor, but it will lie down with him in the dust. 12 "Though evil is sweet in his mouth, though he hides it under his tongue, 13 though he is loath to let it go and holds it in his mouth, 14 yet his food is turned in his stomach; it is the venom of cobras within him. 15 He swallows down riches and vomits them up again; God casts them out of his belly. 16 He will suck the poison of cobras; the tongue of a viper will kill him. 17 He will not look upon the rivers, the streams flowing with honey and curds. 18 He will give back the fruit of his toil and will not swallow it down; from the profit of his trading he will get no enjoyment. 19 For he has crushed and abandoned the poor; he has seized a house that he did not build. 20 "Because he knew no contentment in his belly, he will not let anything in which he delights escape him. 21 There was nothing left after he had eaten; therefore his prosperity will not endure. 22 In the fullness of his sufficiency he will be in distress; the hand of everyone in misery will come against him. 23 To fill his belly to the full, God will send his burning anger against him and rain it upon him into his body.

CHAPTER 9
THE UNBELIEVING UNBELIEVER OR THE FOOL DOES NOT HAVE EARS TO HEAR

The *Unbelieving Unbeliever*
1. Is wicked and a fool
2. Is right in his own eyes
3. Despises understanding and wisdom
4. Speaks destruction to his soul
5. He calls God a liar by his own confession
6. Is violent in nature
7. Does not have spiritual ears to hear

Psalms 94:7-8 (ESV) and they say, "The LORD does not see; the God of Jacob does not perceive." 8 Understand, O dullest of the people! Fools, when will you be wise?

The Hebrew word fool in Psalms 94:8 is "kesiyl," the same as Proverbs 18:2, 18:7, and 29:9. It is translated as stupid or silly. This word is used 70 times in the Old Testament.

The phrase "O dullest of people" is brutish and means waste, such as eating up or burning up. It carries the idea of a wasteful and undisciplined life that misses opportunities to be wise because of living foolishly and gluttonously for the moment. When people become atheists, their hearts become seared. I have seen people who had been burned badly and their skin seared. When it is third-degree burns, it reaches the fat layer beneath the skin. Burned areas may be black, brown, or white, and the skin may look leathery. Third-degree burns can destroy nerves, causing numbness. Some burn victims suffer permanent nerve destruction and related disabilities losing all sensation in the affected area.

1 Timothy 4:2 (ESV) through the insincerity of liars whose consciences are seared,

In chapter 7, we discussed that the *Unbelieving Unbelievers* call God a liar when in effect, they are liars in denying the existence of God. As I discussed earlier, the searing of the nerves happens to someone who has experienced third-degree burns. The same happens to those who reject the truth of God and His Word. They experience searing of the heart. They become unmoved by the Person and presence of the Holy Spirit and can no longer believe that God exists and that Jesus died for them.

It takes the Person of the Holy Spirit to convict someone of sin, righteousness, and judgment. We cannot know that we are sinners, that Jesus Christ is the only truly righteous one, and that there is a judgment of hell for those who reject God's love and grace.

> **John 16:7-11 (ESV) Nevertheless, I tell you the truth: it is to your advantage that I go away, for if I do not go away, the Helper will not come to you. But if I go, I will send him to you. 8 And when he comes, he will convict the world concerning sin and righteousness and judgment: 9 concerning sin, because they do not believe in me; 10 concerning righteousness, because I go to the Father, and you will see me no longer; 11 concerning judgment, because the ruler of this world is judged.**

The Holy Spirit convicts us and reveals the reality of the deity of Jesus Christ. It is the Holy Spirit who takes us to Christ, and it is our Lord Jesus Christ who takes us to the Father. We cannot be saved without coming to the Son for forgiveness.

Is Atheism Dead?

John 14:6 (ESV) Jesus said to him, "I am the way, and the truth, and the life. No one comes to the Father except through me.

Everyone will experience the conviction and wooing of the Holy Spirit sometime in their lives. If people reject the conviction of the Holy Spirit, then they will not believe in the Lord Jesus Christ and reject the Word of God. If they reject Christ and the Word, they will reject the Father. Faith comes by hearing and hearing by the Word of God.

Romans 10:17 (ESV) So faith comes from hearing, and hearing through the word of Christ.

Those who stay in God's Word should rejoice and be greatly encouraged that faith is being matured in us. We should also rejoice that we have ears to hear what the Spirit says to us in the last days.

The *Unbelieving Unbelievers* or atheists don't have any answers for the pressings issues that befall society in our times. They are hopeless without hope. The best they can do is pass more laws trying to force people into some fashion of morality and order while attempting to keep some form of peace and safety in our society. We who believe should

47

stand as men and women with the answers to the perils of today.

CHAPTER 10
THE UNBELIEVING
UNBELIEVER OR THE FOOL
WILL PERISH IN THE ETERNAL
LAKE OF FIRE

The *Unbelieving Unbeliever*
1. Is wicked and a fool
2. Is right in his own eyes
3. Despises understanding and wisdom
4. Speaks destruction to his soul
5. He calls God a liar by his own confession
6. Is violent in nature
7. Does not have spiritual ears to hear
8. Will perish in hell

Psalms 92:5-7 (ESV) How great are your works, O LORD! Your thoughts are very deep! 6 The stupid man cannot know; the fool cannot understand this: 7 that though the wicked sprout like grass and all evildoers flourish, they are doomed to destruction forever;

The Hebrew word fool in Psalms 92:6 is "kesiyl," the same as Psalms 94:8, Proverbs 18:2, 18:7,

49

and 29:9. It is translated as stupid or silly. This word is used 70 times in the Old Testament.

The Hebrew word wicked in Psalms 92:7 is the same as in Psalms 10:4 and 94:3, which we read earlier. The word is "rasha" (H7563) translated as morally wrong, an actively bad person, condemned, guilty, ungodly, and wicked. This word is used 263 times in the Old Testament.

Revelation 21:8 (ESV) But as for the cowardly, the faithless, the detestable, as for murderers, the sexually immoral, sorcerers, idolaters, and all liars, their portion will be in the lake that burns with fire and sulfur, which is the second death."

The Greek word faithless in Revelation 21:8 is the word "apistos" (G571) translated as disbelieving, without Christian faith, a heathen, untrustworthy, and faithless. This word is used 23 times in the New Testament.

We as believers do not have the right or authority from God to tell someone they are going to hell. However, we have the right and responsibility to tell someone what God's Word tells us about the sacrificial atonement of our Lord Jesus Christ and to reject it carries the judgment of hell.

The Scriptures tell us that we will know them by their fruit. The fruit reveals the root. That makes us fruit inspectors. So, we are to judge from the position of *evaluation* according to God's Word. Judging by evaluation is not casting a sentence. Think of it as a jury of twelve listening to the testimony of someone accused of a crime. They evaluate the facts of the evidence only. The jury comes back with a guilty or nonguilty plea based on the evaluation of facts given. Judging by casting a sentence is not the juror's job, nor is it our job. God the Father casts out the sentencing.

> *Matthew 7:15-20 (ESV) "Beware of false prophets, who come to you in sheep's clothing but inwardly are ravenous wolves. 16 You will recognize them by their fruits. Are grapes gathered from thornbushes, or figs from thistles? 17 So, every healthy tree bears good fruit, but the diseased tree bears bad fruit. 18 A healthy tree cannot bear bad fruit, nor can a diseased tree bear good fruit. 19 Every tree that does not bear good fruit is cut down and thrown into the fire. 20 Thus you will recognize them by their fruits.*

CHAPTER 11
WE WERE ALL UNBELIEVING UNBELIEVERS OR FOOLISH AT ONE TIME

The *Unbelieving Unbeliever*
1. Is wicked and a fool
2. Is right in his own eyes
3. Despises understanding and wisdom
4. Speaks destruction to his soul
5. He calls God a liar by his own confession
6. Is violent in nature
7. Does not have spiritual ears to hear
8. Will perish in hell
9. We were all fools at one time before salvation

Titus 3:3-5 (ESV) For we ourselves were once foolish, disobedient, led astray, slaves to various passions and pleasures, passing our days in malice and envy, hated by others and hating one another. 4 But when the goodness and loving kindness of God our Savior appeared, 5 he saved us, not because of works done by us in righteousness, but according to his own mercy, by the washing of

regeneration and renewal of the Holy Spirit,

The Greek word foolish in Titus 3:3 is "anoetos" (G453), translated as unintelligent, unwise, and sensual. This word is used six times in the New Testament. We all started in the same spiritual condition. We were all spiritually lost and without a cue until the Holy Spirit wooed our hearts.

We may have differed in family size, race, sex, culture, financial status, educational opportunities, and spiritual training. However, there is one place that remains the leveler of all humanity. We all started spiritually in need of a Savior. In each of our lives, we battled with the issue of faith and the existence of God. We all fought with the same Adamic sin nature that separated us from God. We all needed to respond to the wooing of the Holy Spirit to receive the gift of salvation offered by our Lord. Before receiving Christ, we all had a time when we were foolish in our hearts. This foolishness many times manifested itself in word, deed, and thought.

The problem is not that we all started out the same. The problem is not with the work of the Holy Spirit convicting the heart of every person who has ever lived. The problem lies in the response once convicted.

The Father is loving and gracious towards us in offering His free gift of salvation through the work of His Son, Jesus Christ. However, He is not under any obligation to make that offer more than once. Those who say no to the Holy Spirit when He is wooing the heart to Jesus are already in danger of having a hardened and seared heart. The story of the Rich Young Ruler is an excellent example of someone who came to the right person, asked the right question, received the right answer, yet made the wrong decision.

> ***Luke 18:18-23 (ESV) And a ruler asked him, "Good Teacher, what must I do to inherit eternal life?" 19 And Jesus said to him, "Why do you call me good? No one is good except God alone. 20 You know the commandments: 'Do not commit adultery, Do not murder, Do not steal, Do not bear false witness, Honor your father and mother.'" 21 And he said, "All these I have kept from my youth." 22 When Jesus heard this, he said to him, "One thing you still lack. Sell all that you have and distribute to the poor, and you will have treasure in heaven; and come, follow me." 23 But when he heard these***

things, he became very sad, for he was extremely rich.

The best example in the New Testament of *Unbelieving Unbelievers* having the Word of God shared with them yet immediately taken is the parable of the four soils. The soils are the different heart conditions of mankind. The first soil is called the "Wayside" soil. It is the path people take either on the edges or through the planted field. The world often travels it. The soil is packed down hard like concrete and cannot receive any seed that might fall on it. In the parable, the seed is called the Word of God, and the sower is Jesus.

First came the parable.

Matthew 13:3-4 (ESV) And he told them many things in parables, saying: "A sower went out to sow. 4 And as he sowed, some seeds fell along the path, and the birds came and devoured them.

Mark 4:3-4 (ESV) "Listen! Behold, a sower went out to sow. 4 And as he sowed, some seed fell along the path, and the birds came and devoured it.

Luke 8:5 (ESV) "A sower went out to sow his seed. And as he sowed,

some fell along the path and was trampled underfoot, and the birds of the air devoured it.

From Matthew 13:3-4, Mark 4:3-4, and Luke 8:5, we know that the sower sowed His seed by spreading it out on all fields. Some of the seeds fell on the well-beaten pathway. First, the seed was trampled underfoot by those passing through. Secondly, all the seed on the path was devoured by the birds.

Then came the interpretation.

Matthew 13:18-19 (ESV) "Hear then the parable of the sower: 19 When anyone hears the word of the kingdom and does not understand it, the evil one comes and snatches away what has been sown in his heart. This is what was sown along the path.

Mark 4:14-15 (ESV) The sower sows the word. 15 And these are the ones along the path, where the word is sown: when they hear, Satan immediately comes and takes away the word that is sown in them.

Luke 8:11-12 (ESV) Now the parable is this: The seed is the word of God. 12 The ones along the path are those

who have heard; then the devil comes and takes away the word from their hearts, so that they may not believe and be saved.

Our Lord Jesus Christ then gave the parable interpretation to benefit those who have spiritual ears to hear. From Matthew 13:18-19, Mark 4:14-15, and Luke 8:11-12, we can see that when God's Word and the Gospel message are proclaimed and not understood and received, the demonic forces come and snatch that Word away. Faith comes by hearing and hearing by the Word of God.

Romans 10:17 (ESV) So faith comes from hearing, and hearing through the word of Christ.

Let's look at this verse in reverse. We do not have spiritual ears to hear if we do not have God's Word. We have no faith if we do not have spiritual ears to hear. If we have no faith, then the gospel message is foolishness.

So here is the process of how a young person under conviction of the Holy Spirit moves from a tender heart to a hardened and seared heart. This teaching is how someone moves from searching for truth to an atheist or an *Unbelieving Unbeliever.*

They come under conviction of the Holy Spirit of sin, righteousness, and judgment according to John 16:8-11. Every person goes through this stage. However, some will say "No" to God and to the conviction of the Holy Spirit. After so many "noes," the heart starts to become calloused, seared, and hardened.

Once the heart is hardened, the conviction of the Holy Spirit is no longer realized. The heart becomes gospel hardened like the wayward path that had been trampled by the feet of the world. The Word of God is still spread out to the hardened and seared heart, but it is trampled underfoot, mocked, and immediately snatched away by the enemy. With a place for the Word to land and seed, the person no longer has spiritual ears to hear. Without spiritual ears to hear, there is no longer faith. Oh, the atheists may say they have faith. But it is no more than worldly hope like we would say when we remark that we hope it will rain tomorrow. It is little more than wishful thinking.

Without faith, without hope, and without the Word of God, atheists can only rely on their intellect and reasoning. This deduction takes us back to the list of traits of **Unbelieving Unbelievers** that we have covered up to this point. God calls them wicked and fools who despise understanding and wisdom. They speak their own destruction by their confession while calling God a liar. They make themselves liars. They are violent in nature and only need opportunity and the right circumstance. They do not have spiritual ears to hear and, unless they repent, will spend eternity in hell under the judgment of God.

What can we learn from this, and how does it affect us? We need to remain teachable by the Holy Spirit in the things pertaining to life and godliness.

> **2 Peter 1:3-4 (ESV) His divine power has granted to us all things that pertain to life and godliness, through the knowledge of him who called us to his own glory and excellence, 4 by which he has granted to us his precious and very great promises, so that through them you may become partakers of the divine nature, having escaped from the corruption that is in the world because of sinful desire.**

Our Lord commands us to maintain spiritual ears to hear, and we do this by staying in His Word and doing His will. We have a great promise in doing these things. The Lord said that those who have spiritual truth by obedience to His Word would receive even more. To those who do not have ears to hear and do not have spiritual truth, even the things they have will be taken and given to those who already have an abundance.

> *Matthew 13:9 (ESV) He who has ears, let him hear."*
>
> *Mark 4:9 (ESV) And he said, "He who has ears to hear, let him hear."*
>
> *Matthew 13:11-13 (ESV) And he answered them, "To you it has been given to know the secrets of the kingdom of heaven, but to them it has not been given. 12 For to the one who has, more will be given, and he will have an abundance, but from the one who has not, even what he has will be taken away. 13 This is why I speak to them in parables, because seeing they do not see, and hearing they do not hear, nor do they understand.*

CHAPTER 12
THE UNBELIEVING
UNBELIEVER OR THE FOOL
HAS THE SPIRIT OF
ANTICHRIST

The *Unbelieving Unbeliever*
1. Is wicked and a fool
2. Is right in his own eyes
3. Despises understanding and wisdom
4. Speaks destruction to his soul
5. He calls God a liar by his own confession
6. Is violent in nature
7. Does not have spiritual ears to hear
8. Will perish in hell
9. We were all fools at one time before salvation
10. The spirit of antichrist controls them.

1 John 2:18-19 (ESV) Children, it is the last hour, and as you have heard that antichrist is coming, so now many antichrists have come. Therefore we know that it is the last hour. 19 They went out from us, but they were not of us; for if they had been of us, they would have continued with us. But they went out,

***that it might become plain that they
all are not of us.***

People as a whole are temperamental about names or classifications. This attitude is really true among those who are spiritually lost. Those who are spiritually lost have redefined or renamed many things the Bible calls sin over the years. This redefining sin attempts to remove the stigma of it being classified as sin or morally wrong.

The Bible speaks a lot about the sin of drunkenness. Our society renamed it alcoholism and classified it as a disease like it is something you catch, like the common cold or flu.

The Bible speaks a lot about the sanctity of life. Our society renamed the killing of our unborn to abortion and classified it as pro-choice in an attempt to make heroes of those who would kill the unborn.

The Bible speaks a lot about different sexual sins. Our society took perverted sexual sins and renamed them and heralded them before us like they are a banner of progress. Any teachings or comments against fornication and adultery are viewed as old-fashion and extremist. The sins related to homosexual sins are classified as being gay.

Is Atheism Dead?

The trafficking of women and young boys and girls as sex slaves is the most lucrative business globally. It is all about supply and demand.

What has all of this to do with *Unbelieving Unbelievers* or the atheists? Without the knowledge of God and His Word, there remains only one absolute, and that is, there are no absolutes. If humanity embraces a world with no absolutes, then morality becomes amoral, and everyone does what is right in their own eyes. Each person, community, state, or country establishes its own laws to determine what would be called acceptable or unacceptable behavior. However, the idea of classifying behavior as good versus evil or moral versus sinful would be taboo. It would socially and culturally be either acceptable or unacceptable.

Now here is where we get back to renaming or reclassifying certain things. According to 1 John 2:18-19, the *Unbelieving Unbeliever* has the spirit of the antichrist. Those who walk in the spirit of antichrist would be slow to call themselves that. They might classify themselves as intellectuals or progressive. However, the Word of God calls them how God the Father sees them, antichrists.

Those who walk with the spirit of antichrist have always existed. God's Word tells us that these antichrists are among us now. Notice as you read the Scriptures from 1 John 2 that the antichrists came out from among the believers. They hardened their hearts and left the circle of believers.

Notice in 1 John 2 that the antichrists started out in the faith. They were a part of the gathering of true believers, but they departed from the faith. Those who departed did not just backslide. They ultimately turned their back on God and the Lord Jesus Christ and became antichrists. The antichrist denies that Jesus is God. Those who reject Jesus as God also deny God the Father.

1 John 2:22-23 (ESV) Who is the liar but he who denies that Jesus is the Christ? This is the antichrist, he who denies the Father and the Son. 23 No one who denies the Son has the Father. Whoever confesses the Son has the Father also.

1 John 2:22-23 continues that the *Unbelieving Unbeliever* is a liar and has the spirit of antichrist.

2 John 1:7 (ESV) For many deceivers have gone out into the world, those who do not confess the coming of Jesus Christ in the flesh. Such a one is the deceiver and the antichrist.

Is Atheism Dead?

The apostle John continues this thought in 2 John 1:7. Anyone who denies that God came in the flesh in the person of Jesus Christ is a deceiver or liar and has the spirit of antichrist.

1 John 4:1-3 (ESV) Beloved, do not believe every spirit, but test the spirits to see whether they are from God, for many false prophets have gone out into the world. 2 By this you know the Spirit of God: every spirit that confesses that Jesus Christ has come in the flesh is from God, 3 and every spirit that does not confess Jesus is not from God. This is the spirit of the antichrist, which you heard was coming and now is in the world already.

Anyone who does not teach the Biblical truth concerning the deity of Christ is a false prophet. 1 John 4:1-3 tells us to test the spirits and then instructs us how to do so. This testing will identify if the spirit is the Holy Spirit witnessing through the believer or if the antichrist spirit is witnessing through the *Unbelieving Unbeliever.*

1 John 4:1-3 should be very encouraging to us who believe. First, we have the warning not to believe what they say. We are to test the

65

spirit behind the person to see who is operating or driving their behavior. We can know if the voice we hear is a message from God or a false message from the enemy. If the voice speaking denies the deity of our Lord Jesus Christ, then it is the spirit of antichrist.

CHAPTER 13
CLOSING THOUGHTS

H ow do I close the book like this? Even as I was writing this book, a well-known son of one of our former presidents appeared on national TV announcing the formation of an atheist club. He was applauded as the news media was excited to announce this new venture. This example is not the only organization recognizing atheism in America.

The Bible warns us that Christians will face tribulations, trials, and persecution in the last days. The Scriptures say we will be beaten and cast out of our churches while the atheists proclaim across the land "there is no God."

Matthew 24 is an excellent chapter to read, revealing the end-time trials and tribulations Christians face.

One of the faults believers make is thinking that anyone can be our friend. Scriptures are clear about who our friends are and who our enemies are. The Scriptures tell us that we are to love our enemies. To love our enemies, we need to know who they are. We need to understand what Biblically classifies someone as an enemy. Anyone who loves the world and the things of the world is an enemy to God. Those who stand against the virgin birth, life, death, and resurrection of our Lord Jesus Christ are enemies to God, to the cross, to our Savior, to the Holy Spirit, and should be to us. How can we declare someone is our friend who is an enemy to God, to Christ, and stands as an enemy to the work of the cross?

When Jesus said that some of our enemies would be members of our own household, why do we insist on placing biological blood relatives above God's Word? The closest friends that we will ever have are our Lord Jesus Christ and those who follow Him. They will lay their lives down for us. Those who deny Christ will one day betray us no matter how close they seem in relationship to us at this time.

Is atheism dead? No! Atheism is alive and well in the kingdom of darkness. Do not fear, my brothers and sisters, for we are members and citizens of another kingdom. We belong to the kingdom of God, the realm of the light. And we must believe that greater is He that is in us than he that is in the world. We shall overcome, which is why we're called overcomers.

Jesus told us to have peace. He said that we would have trouble in this world, but to take heart because He has overcome the world. It is not that our answer is coming in the sky by and by one day. Our solution has already come. We already have the victory. We can already stand in the position of peace. Is atheism dead? No. But know this. Although the spirit of darkness and the spirit of the antichrist roams the earth creating chaos and releasing lawlessness, the Spirit of the living God has also been poured out upon us. The manifested sons and daughters of God have risen to the occasion, and we shall not be moved. We will not bow, we will not bend, and we will not burn. All for the glory of God. Amen.

MORE BOOKS BY CHARLES MORRIS

Look for *eBooks* (EB), *paperbacks* (PB), & *hardcovers* (HC)

1. *The Four Positions of the Holy Spirit*: Beside Us, Within Us, Upon Us, and Filling Us (EB, PB, HC, 1st, 2nd, & 3rd Editions).
2. *Born Again:* Having a Personal Relationship with God (EB, PB, HC, 1st & 2nd Editions).
3. *The 10 Characteristics of a Spirit-Filled Church:* The Spirit-Filled Life Bible Study (EB, PB, HC 1st Edition).
4. *The Covenant of Salt:* Everyone Will Be Salted with Fire (EB, PB, HC, 1st Edition).
5. *The Parable of the Four Soils:* The Key to the Mystery of the Kingdom of God (EB, PB, HC, 1st Edition).
6. *The Five Evidences of Salvation:* How Do I Know That I'm Saved (EB, PB, HC, 1st & 2nd Editions).
7. *Faithful:* How Can I Be Faithful to God? (EB, PB, HC, 1st & 2nd Editions).
8. *HOSEA:* What Does the Book of Hosea Teach Us? (EB, PB, HC, 1st Edition).
9. *Preparing Ourselves to Hear the Voice*

of God: Do You Want to Hear the Voice of God? Book 1 (EB, PB, HC, 1st & 2nd Editions).

10. *Fifteen Ways to Hear the Voice of God:* Do You Want to Hear the Voice of God? Book 2 (EB, PB, HC, 1st & 2nd Editions).

11. *The 24 Qualifications of an Elder:* What Are the Biblical Requirements to Be an Elder? (EB, PB, HC, 1st Edition).

12. *The Bible Proves Itself True* (EB, PB, HC, 1st Edition).

13. *Experiencing the Beauty of Brokenness:* You Shall Be a Crown of Beauty in the Hand of the Lord, and a Royal Diadem in the Hand of Your God (PB, 1st Edition).

14. *Places Where God and Man Meet:* A Guide to Worshipping in Spirit & Truth (EB, PB, HC, 1st Edition).

15. *Your Dash:* Writing Your Life Journal (PB, 1st & 2nd Edition).

16. *Chart Your Path:* Bible Study Journal (PB, 1st & 2nd Editions).

17. *The Five Witnesses of Salvation:* You Shall Know The By Their Fruit (EB, PB, HC, 1st Edition).

18. *How Do I Write a Book?* From Passion to Paper to Print (EB, PB, HC, 1st Edition).

19. *HOSEA Introduction:* Can You Still Hear the Call? (EB, 1st Edition).

20. *HOSEA 1:1-3:* The Divine Command to Marry Gomer (EB, 1ˢᵗ Edition).
21. *HOSEA 1:4-5:* A Marriage, A Son, and the Promise of Judgment (EB, 1ˢᵗ Edition).
22. *HOSEA 1:6-7:* A Daughter, an Unfaithful Wife, Heartbreak, and No Mercy (EB, 1ˢᵗ Edition).
23. *HOSEA 1:8-9:* A Son, You Are Not My People, I Am Not Your God. (EB, 1ˢᵗ Edition).
24. *HOSEA 1:10-11:* The Ultimate Promise: Divine Intervention And Restoration. (EB, 1ˢᵗ Edition).
25. *A Willingness To Be Taught:* Overcoming The Dull Of Hearing Syndrome. (EB, PB, HC, 1ˢᵗ Edition).
26. *LUKE 15:* The Sheep, A Wandering Heart; The Coin, A Careless Heart; The Son, A Rebellious Heart. (EB, PB, 1ˢᵗ Edition).
27. *The Mystery Of Lawlessness.* (EB, PB, HC, 1ˢᵗ Edition).

ABOUT THE AUTHOR

Over the last 45 years, CHARLES MORRIS has served God and the body of Christ as a pastor, church planter, evangelist, house church ministry coordinator, and author of over 20 books. He is also the founder and CEO of RSIM (Raising the Standard International Ministry), RSIP (Raising the Standard International Publishing LLC), and RSISoM (Raising the Standard International School of Ministry).

Pastor Charles has devoted his life, talents, gifts, and resources to call the church to maturity and back to the place of walking in God's holiness in the power of the Holy Spirit. He calls on the living body of Christ on the earth (the church) to live a daily Christ-like life in word, deed, and thought.

Pastor Charles believes that it is paramount that all who confess to know Christ have a full assurance that they are genuinely saved by examining their lives according to the standards set within God's Word. After proof of salvation, he also believes all Christians be a bold witness for our Lord Jesus Christ across the street and to the ends of the earth.

Charles currently lives with his wife, Debra, in Navarre, Florida.

Made in the USA
Middletown, DE
03 November 2022

14068613R00046